MW01599080

Tigers

NATURE'S PREDATORS

Stuart P. Levine

KIDHAVEN PRESS

THOMSON
™
GALE

Detroit • New York • San Diego • San Francisco
Boston • New Haven, Conn. • Waterville, Maine
London • Munich

Picture Credits

Cover Credit: © Mitsuaki Iwago/Minden Pictures
© AFP/CORBIS, 10
Associated Press, AP, 42
© Tom Brakefield/CORBIS, 34
© Christie's Images/CORBIS, 36 (top)
© Bryn Colton/Assignments Photographers/CORBIS, 12
© Richard A. Cooke/CORBIS, 36 (bottom)
Corel Stock Photo Library, 21, 30
© William Dow/CORBIS, 19
© Frank Lane Picture Agency/CORBIS, 4, 14
© D. Robert and Lorri Franz/CORBIS, 15
© Getty Images, 17
© Peter Johnson/CORBIS, 25
Chris Jouan, 7, 9, 32, 38
© Joe McDonald/CORBIS, 22
© Enzo and Paolo Ragazzini/CORBIS, 40
© Keren Su/CORBIS, 24, 29
© Konrad Wothe/Minden Pictures, 39
© Shin Yoshino/Minden Pictures, 27

Library of Congress Cataloging-in-Publication Data

Levine, Stuart P., 1968–
  Tigers / by Stuart P. Levine.
    p. cm. — (Nature's predators)
  Includes bibliographical references (p.   ).
  Summary: Discusses tiger behavior, hunting practices and diet, and the threats they face from humans.
    ISBN 0-7377-1007-1 (hardback : alk. paper)
  1. Tigers—Juvenile literature. [1. Tigers. 2. Endangered species.] I. Title. II. Series.
  QL737.C23 L475 2002
  599.756—dc21

                              2002005692

Contents

Chapter 1

Beautiful but Deadly

The tiger is one of the most beautiful creatures in nature. The soft fur, big eyes, and stunning orange-and-black-striped coat make the tiger look like a giant stuffed toy. Its looks, however, are deceiving. There is nothing cuddly about a tiger, especially when it is hungry. It is one of the fiercest predators on earth and has earned its place at the top of the **food chain**.

The tiger is a distant cousin to all other cats, from lions and leopards to the common house cat. The tiger is the largest of all the cats—reaching weights of more than seven hundred pounds—and needs to eat an enormous amount of food. It can eat up to sixty pounds of meat in one sitting. In general, cats are some of the only truly carnivorous, or meat eating, land animals. Even wolves and bears will eat some vegetation. Cats, though, will eat only meat. The food the tiger hunts for is called **prey**. The tiger will usually hunt for animals such as deer and pigs, though it sometimes goes after prey as large as buffalo and even young rhinos and elephants!

Where in the World?

All tigers live in Asia and most live in the dense jungle. Some, however, live in the cold Siberian forests of northern Russia. In fact, scientists think that millions of years ago, the tiger originated in that area. Over time, they migrated, or traveled, south and west until they inhabited nearly all of Asia from Turkey to Korea, and as far south as the Indonesian islands. As they moved apart from each other, tigers that lived in these different areas began to look a little different from each other. Today, these differences have become important enough that scientists call some of them by different names. There are Siberian tigers that still live in Russia, as well as Sumatran tigers, which live on only one island off the southern coast of Asia. Once a total of eight different types of tigers lived in the world, but some of these have disappeared and only five remain. By far, the most plentiful of the tigers is the Bengal tiger, found in and around India. There are between four and five thousand Bengal tigers left in the world. Although the tiger may have originated in the cold north, today most of them live in very hot, humid forests.

The Lazy Life of a Tiger

During the daytime, it is far too hot in the Asian jungle for predator or prey to move around much,

Range of the Tiger

RUSSIA

Caspian Sea

CHINA

KOREA

Siberian Tiger

Caspian Tiger (extinct)

Indo-Chinese Tiger

South China Tiger

INDIA

MYANMAR

THAILAND

Bengal Tiger

Javan Tiger (extinct)

Sumatran Tiger

Bali Tiger (extinct)

SUMATRA

JAVA   BALI

Range around 1900
Estimated current range

so the tiger spends most of its day lounging around in the shade, resting or sleeping. Unlike other cats, tigers will cool off in the water. Most cats do not like the water, but tigers love it. In fact, they can often be seen lounging in rivers or even splashing around for play. They are natural swimmers and can manage just as well in water as on land. They have been seen swimming up to three miles at a time without any rest at all. In some parts of India and Southeast Asia, they spend so much time in the water that scientists consider them **semiaquatic**. In fact, they are so comfortable in the water that they usually have a much better chance of catching their prey when chasing it through water than on land.

In general, the heat of the day keeps the tiger from moving around too much. However, the night is not a good time for hunting either because it is much too dark for the tiger to locate its prey. The only time the tiger becomes fully awake and ready to hunt is in the evening, just as the sun begins to set, or in the morning, just as it begins to rise. The tiger is **crepuscular**, which means it is active only at dusk and dawn.

What Does It Eat?

The tiger goes after many different types of food. It typically hunts prey that is small enough to take down but big enough to provide a decent meal. However, when it is hungry, the tiger will take advantage of any opportunity for a meal. So, in addition to deer, it will occasionally eat rodents, crabs, frogs, birds, and even fish. When they are very hungry or very brave, tigers have even been known to go after such animals as young elephants or rhinos.

In India, its favorite prey is a sambar deer. These deer can weigh nearly seven hundred pounds, which is twice the size of some tigers. Other prey, like the chital deer, is much smaller but very fast and nimble. Although the tiger is one of the world's best hunters, it does not have an easy time catching its food. In nature, most animals have **adaptations**, or behaviors or parts of their bodies, that help them to survive. The prey animals are well adapted to avoid being caught. They often have excellent eyesight and hearing, they can be very fast, and sometimes they are very large. Fortunately for the tiger, it also has many adaptations that help it to survive. In many ways, the tiger is the perfect predator. It is the strongest of all the cats. It can often knock down prey more than twice its own size using the force of its massive body.

The tiger also has powerful legs for jumping and special muscles on its jaw and head that give its mouth strong crushing power. Its canine teeth are long and sharp. They use these teeth to grab onto and hold their prey. Like all cats, tigers have

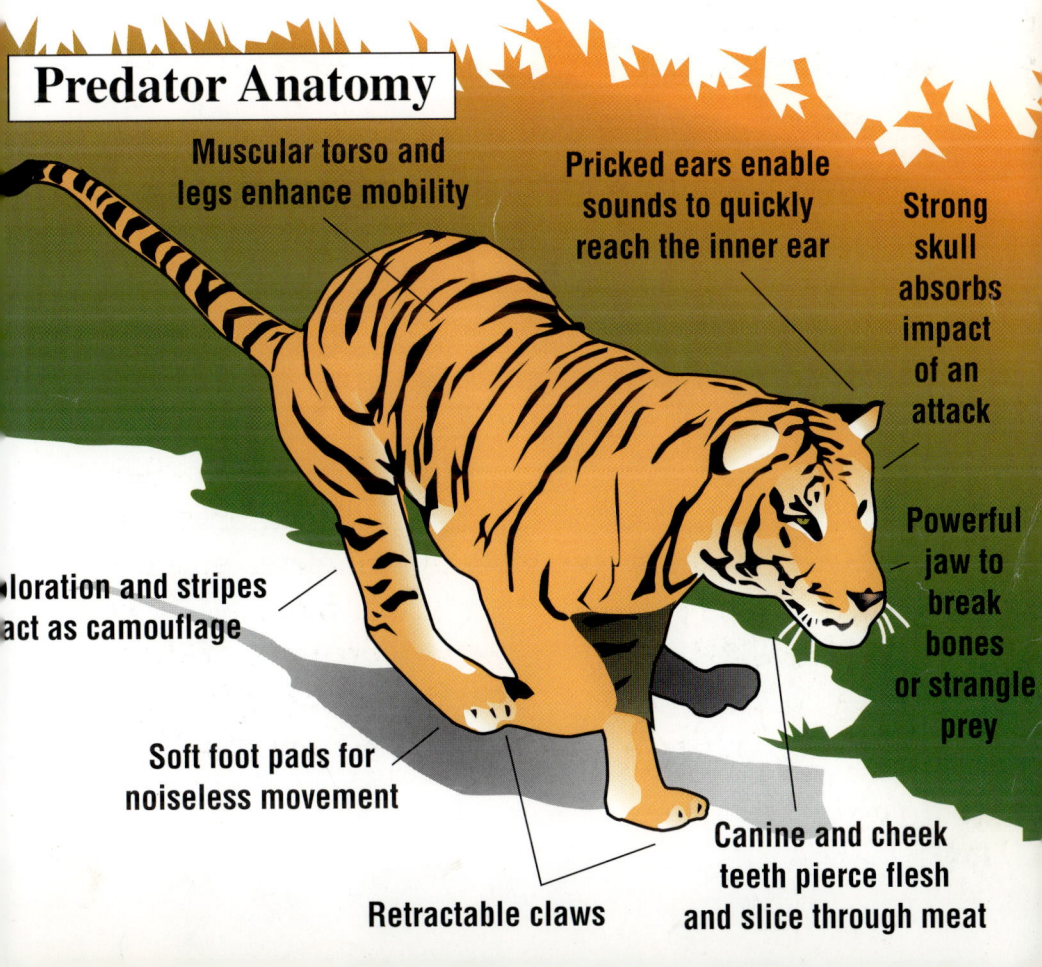

Predator Anatomy

Muscular torso and legs enhance mobility

Pricked ears enable sounds to quickly reach the inner ear

Strong skull absorbs impact of an attack

Powerful jaw to break bones or strangle prey

loration and stripes act as camouflage

Soft foot pads for noiseless movement

Retractable claws

Canine and cheek teeth pierce flesh and slice through meat

retractable claws. This means that, unlike a dog, their claws stay up inside their paws unless they push them out. This way, the claws do not get worn down on the rough forest floor as they walk. A tiger's claws are always sharp and can be used as weapons in the hunt.

The Invisible Cat

One of the tiger's most important features is its ability to move unseen and unheard through the forest. It has a number of adaptations to help with this. The soft pads on its feet help to keep its steps from being heard. Its body is low to the ground, so

A tiger's orange-and-black-striped coat helps it blend in with its environment.

it can walk in a crouched position for as long as it needs to stay hidden. The tiger also uses its fur coat to stay hidden. The tiger's bright orange-and-black-striped coat seems as though it would stand out like a brightly colored flag in the forest. As it turns out, this coloration helps it hide. Because the tiger hunts only at dawn and at dusk, there are always long shadows throughout the forest. The orange color helps the tiger to blend in with the pinkish orange sunlight that bathes the forest in the early morning and evening. The black stripes help to break up the shape of its body, so if it sits very still, it looks like a part of the forest, all shadows and sunlight. Each tiger's stripe pattern is completely unique, or different, from any other tiger in the world. This pattern is like a human fingerprint. While the stripes may all look pretty similar to us, tigers can tell the difference and this is sometimes how they recognize friends and enemies.

Family Life

Although tigers do live near each other in the wild and need to be able to recognize their neighbors, they are not very social animals. Unlike their African cousins, the lions, which live in large family groups, tigers are basically solitary creatures. They like to live by themselves, keeping their neighbors at a comfortable distance. The only time tigers can be found living together in the wild is when a mother is raising her young. She will have

A mother tiger licks her cub's coat, cleaning dirt from its fur.

anywhere from one to five cubs at a time; she takes very good care of them, cleaning them, feeding them, and protecting them. The mother keeps her cubs with her for up to two years, but after that they are on their own. Living a solitary lifestyle means that they cannot rely on others for help when hunting. They have to bear that burden on their own. As a result, the tiger has developed some first-class techniques for catching its prey.

Chapter 2

The Silent Hunt

With its strength, speed, and built-in weapons, the tiger is a superb predator. Its instincts, or the skills it is born with, help it to be so successful. However, instincts are not enough. Many of the tactics used by the tiger must be learned. For example, a very young tiger can often be seen attempting to chase down birds or small animals over great distances. It is never successful because it has not yet learned that tigers do not hunt that way. They are not distance runners and must, instead, stalk their prey, pouncing on it at the last moment. Young tigers must learn from their mothers how to hunt.

Home Schooling

Female tigers have a difficult job in the wild. Not only must they take care of themselves and live their lives in a continual search for food, but they must also devote a lot of time to teaching their young to hunt and survive. They must do this alone because the male tiger is never an active participant in the schooling.

Newborn cubs nurse from their mother's milk.

When her cubs are first born, she must nurse them frequently. However, to produce so much milk, she must also eat a lot. So the mother will typically hide her cubs in deep brush for several hours each day while she goes out to look for a meal for herself. Once the cubs are old enough to eat on their own, she will usually drag part of a **carcass** back to her hiding spot and let them eat their fill.

The mother tiger will play with her cubs to help teach them some of the basics of the hunt. Games such as hide and seek and tail chasing help them gain the coordination they will need to pounce on real prey later in life.

Once the day arrives that they can move around quite well on their own, she will take them out to watch her hunt. In the beginning, they are so excited by this that they run and jump and play with each other. Unfortunately, this noise scares away the prey and the mother is unable to hunt. So she spends a good amount of time teaching them one of the hardest, and most important, lessons they ever learn: to stay quiet. The mother will growl at the cubs or swat them with her paw if they make any noise while observing a hunt. The cubs watch and learn from

Two tiger cubs practice stalking by walking silently with slow, precise steps.

their mother. As they grow older, she will sometimes injure a deer or other prey and then let the
cubs finish it off. This practice helps lead up to
the day when they will have to hunt on their own.

Distant Neighbors

Once they are old enough, strong enough, and
skilled enough to catch their own food, usually
around two years of age, the mother tiger will
typically send her youngsters out into the world
on their own. Sometimes they do this by themselves and sometimes she must force them away
against their will. Once they leave the protection
of their mother, they must wander around and es-
tablish a territory for themselves.

A tiger's territory is the section of forest in
which they live and hunt. It is similar to what people might consider their neighborhood. Just like a
person has an actual house within the neighborhood, the tiger has one small part of the territory
that it spends most of its time in. This is known as
its home range. Several tigers may share or over-
lap territories, but none are usually tolerated
within another's home range.

The tiger must defend its territory from
neighboring tigers to prevent them from coming
in and eating all their prey. Tigers will typically
mark the outskirts of their territory by urinating
and leaving claw marks on trees. A tiger's urine
smells very strong and the scent can linger for
days or even weeks. When other tigers come

across this smell, they will approach the tree and wrinkle their nose up while they inhale. This tells the tiger exactly who left the mark there. They can read it as easily as a person can read a signature. If they know the local tiger and are on good terms with it, they may venture a little farther in to see if they can find some food. The closer they get to the home range, the more markings they will find. And if they get too close, the resident tiger may chase the visiting tiger out.

Young tigers may have a difficult time establishing their own territory. They may have to travel many miles before they find an unoccupied stretch of forest. Or, if they are brave enough, they may try to force one of the resident tigers out of their current territory and take it over for themselves.

Two tigers fight over territory.

The Lay of the Land

Living and hunting in the same area all the time is a crucial part of the tiger's survival. They know their territory and especially their home range very well. Tigers study the behavior patterns of the creatures that live in their territory. They learn where prey hides, as well as where and when prey eats, sleeps, and drinks. It even learns how these behavior patterns change over the seasons. By learning about its prey, it can more easily capture it.

The Tiger's Senses

The job of capturing prey is not an easy one. The tiger must rely on its well-developed senses to accomplish this task. Its eyesight is very good but only in certain conditions. It is not always able to see another animal, even when that animal is standing perfectly still. However, it can always detect movement. It is also able to see very well in low-light conditions. Like most cats, it has a special layer of cells in its eyes called the **tapetum.** The tapetum is very sensitive to light and helps the cat see objects even when just a small amount of light is available. This special reflective layer is what causes a cat's eyes to shine in the dark. By hunting during dawn and dusk, the tiger has an advantage over the animals it hunts. Most of the tiger's prey cannot see very well at these times of the day.

Although the tiger may use its sense of smell to detect the territories of other tigers, this is not one of its most highly developed senses. Its hearing, on the other hand, is probably its best sense. Tigers can detect the slightest sounds in the forest and even tell the difference between the sounds made by different types of animals walking through the forest. They will typically ignore the

A special layer of cells in the eye allow the tiger to see in the dark.

sounds of animals they are not interested in, but they will perk right up when they hear a favorite snack walking nearby.

Stealth Mode

The tiger's most important feature when hunting is silence. If even one prey animal sees the tiger on the move, it will send out an alarm call to alert every creature in the area. The sambar deer have a very distinctive "honk" that researchers will sometimes use to help them locate tigers.

Fortunately, the tiger is naturally stealthy. Its amazing grace allows it to glide along unseen and unheard. It will move both legs on one side of its body at the same time and then move the other pair right afterward. Studies of the tiger's movements have shown that there is a mathematical precision to their step. The pads on their paws are large and soft enough to help absorb the cat's massive weight and cushion its impact on the ground. However, these soft pads also prevent the tiger from moving across certain types of rocky terrain. If the rocks are too sharp or too hot from the sun, it will hurt the tiger's feet. The tiger's prey, such as deer, often have tough hooves that do not have this kind of sensitivity. They will use this to their advantage and travel across rocky terrain whenever possible, avoiding tigers in the process.

Stalking

Tigers have a number of methods they will use to capture their prey. One of the easiest is to simply lie in wait by a watering hole in the evening when animals typically come to drink. During dry seasons the watering holes may be too small to attract large numbers of animals. Tigers may have to get more creative and wander through the forest looking for unwary prey.

In either case, once it spots its prey it begins to do what cats do best: stalk. It crouches its body low to the ground and uses all its natural abilities to slowly and quietly move toward the unsuspecting prey. The entire time it is moving, it keeps its eyes focused on its target. It will occasionally raise and lower its head to judge the animal's distance and direction. After getting as close as it can without being seen, the tiger

A tiger crouches as it stalks its prey.

makes some final calculations and then launches from its hiding spot. It leaps directly toward its prey, hoping to catch it on the first try. If it misses, it will bounce off the ground, almost instantly changing direction toward the prey, and leap again. It may even try a third leap if necessary. However, after three unsuccessful leaps, the tiger will typically give up. By this time, the deer or other prey has had a chance to flee and the tiger knows that it is no match for a deer in an open run.

The hunt is no easy task, even for a tiger. It is usually successful in catching its prey only about

A young tiger will have to try again after it fails to capture its prey.

one out of every twenty attempts. Because this is the only way the tiger gets a meal, it ends up spending most of its waking hours hunting. It may go several days at a time with nothing to eat. So, once it does capture its prey, the tiger does a very quick and efficient job of killing it.

Chapter 3

The Meal

Once the tiger has successfully captured its prey, it has only a short time to make the kill. The prey animal will fight with every ounce of strength it has to escape. If the tiger is not careful, it will lose its meal.

Tigers have a few different methods of subduing or killing their prey. Typically, they will attempt to launch themselves onto the other animal from behind. If necessary they will sometimes come at the prey from the side or even the front. In some cases, the force of several hundred pounds of tiger landing on it is enough to kill the prey. Most often, though, they will have to employ the use of their powerful arsenal of weapons to finish the job.

Size Matters

The method the tiger uses to kill will depend on the size of the prey it is attacking. If the prey is small, like a chital deer, the tiger gets the job done in seconds. Once it lands on the deer, the tiger will pull it down and press its sharp claws

Powerful jaws allow the tiger to snap the neck of a stray sheep before settling down to eat.

into the animal's head and shoulders. It uses this grip to quickly bend the head down and expose the neck. If this snapping action is not enough to instantly break its neck, the tiger will then sink its long, powerful canine teeth into the deer's neck and attempt to sever the spinal column. Once this happens, the deer dies very quickly.

If the tiger is going after something larger, such as a sambar deer, it may not be able to snap its neck or get through the tough skin and muscle on the back of the neck. Instead, it will usually try something different. After knocking it down, the tiger may swing around the front of the sambar's neck and clamp down on its windpipe, or **trachea**, with its vicelike jaws. This kind of deer is very large and may put up quite a fight, but if the tiger is strong enough and persistent enough, it will hold on until the deer eventually suffocates.

Special Tactics

On occasion, a tiger will go after prey that seems almost too big. It is not completely out of the question to see a tiger take down a young rhino or elephant. In this case, the tiger will find a herd of these animals and begin to slowly and carefully circle it. Elephants, for example, are very social creatures and will fiercely protect any member of

A herd of elephants keeps the youngest in the center of the group, away from possible danger.

their group from predators, so the tiger must be careful. It will observe everything about the herd's movements, identifying the youngest or weakest animal in the group. It waits patiently for its chance.

Eventually, one young elephant may wander off by itself a short distance from the herd. This is the tiger's chance to strike. It will move in quickly and launch itself at the animal. Even a young elephant is much too big for a tiger to tackle in the ordinary manner. So instead, the tiger will put out its sharp claws and slash through the elephant's hamstring, a muscle that runs along the back of the ankle. Once the hamstring is cut, the animal can barely walk on that leg.

The cries of the injured animal will draw its family over and the tiger makes a speedy exit. Now, all the tiger has to do is follow and wait. This type of injury will slow the elephant down considerably as it tries to walk. It will have great difficulty keeping up with the herd. The strain of walking will continue to worsen the condition and eventually, the elephant will fall behind completely. When this happens, the tiger is free to move in again. It may slice another hamstring to bring the helpless creature all the way to its knees. Then it will go in for the kill.

Table for One

Typically, the tiger will not eat its prey where it killed it. Instead, the tiger will drag the prey off

Avoiding other predators, a tiger drags a sambar deer backward through the forest.

to a secluded spot where it can eat in peace. There are plenty of other predators in the forest that might be hungry enough to try stealing the tiger's hard-won meal. With smaller prey, the tiger will carry it forward, letting it drag between its own front legs. If the prey is too large, the tiger will get a good hold of it and pull it backward. This is another example of the tiger's enormous strength. They may have to drag the carcass a very long distance before they feel safe enough to eat it. Tigers have been seen dragging their prey as far as a mile. Their strength is amazing. They do not just drag off smaller prey; they will pull even a young rhino or buffalo into cover before eating it. In fact, scientists say that one large tiger has the pulling strength of thirty men, even though it may weigh as much as only four or five men.

Never Waste Any Food

The tiger will eat nearly every part of the carcass, but it takes some time to prepare the food. It will remove the hair and skin and then tear open a section of the carcass to get to the organs. It will usually begin with the major organs such as the heart, liver, or kidneys. The stomach and intestines are usually the only part that is not eaten because it may contain partially digested food and waste materials.

After the nutrient-rich organs have been eaten, the tiger will begin on the muscle. This is the part a person would think of as "meat," similar to a raw steak. They use their claws to hold down the carcass as they pull it apart with their powerful teeth. Their tongue is very rough, like sandpaper, and they use it to lick every last scrap of meat from the bone.

Tigers are very quiet and serious eaters. It can take them an hour or more to eat and they can swallow anywhere from forty to ninety pounds in just one sitting. That is the equivalent of several hundred hamburgers.

Leftovers

If there is still food left over after the tiger is full, it will save it for later. However, it must be careful not

Using its claws to hold the carcass, a tiger rips away flesh with its powerful teeth.

to let others find its stash of food. Crows and vultures circling overhead will often give away the carcass's location to other predators. The tiger will try to prevent this by covering up the carcass with leaves, grasses, and mud. Once the food has been stashed, the tiger can go off to drink and nap.

When it comes back, it may find that others have discovered its hidden meal. If it is just a single

After a large meal, a tiger relaxes and naps on the shaded forest ground.

wild dog or a young tiger, the fierce cat will chase them off and settle back down to finish its meal. However, if the competing tiger is big enough, or if there are a pack of wild dogs, the tiger may choose to give up the carcass in search of other prey. One large kill can last a tiger up to two days. After they have had their fill, they will not do much over the next few days but lay around, digesting and relaxing. It may be several days before the tiger begins to hunt again, but once it is hungry, it gets right back to the only job it has ever known: the hunt.

Chapter 4

When the Hunter Is Hunted

Every plant, animal, and bacteria has its place in the world. This is sometimes referred to as the circle of life. Herbivores are animals that eat strictly plant material. Carnivores eat the herbivores. The bacteria eat the carnivores after they have died, and the waste products of the bacteria feed the plants. Thus, the circle is complete. Where does the tiger fit in to this cycle?

Good to Be the King

The tiger is at the top of the food chain, or pecking order. It preys on many other creatures, but there are no animals that eat tigers as a primary food source. Much like the lion in Africa, they are the kings of the Asian jungle. Although no other animals regularly feed on tigers, some animals can occasionally pose a threat to them. Crocodiles, for example, have been known to kill tigers. The tiger loves to wade and hunt in the water but

The Food Chain

if it is not careful, every now and then a hungry crocodile will take its chances and try to kill it. The tiger will certainly put up a good fight, but crocodiles have very strong jaws and sharp teeth. If the crocodile manages to pull the tiger under the water, it may very well win itself a royal meal. Wild dogs have also been known to occasionally kill a tiger. By itself, a wild dog is no match for a tiger. However, unlike tigers, these dogs are very social and always hunt in groups, called packs. If a large enough pack goes after a tiger, it will be a long and bloody battle. In the end, depending on how strong the tiger is, it may lose the battle and become a meal for the dogs to share. Typically, in these cases the dogs will go after a tiger that appears very old, very sick, or very young.

New Kid on the Block

The biggest threat to tigers comes when they are young. The survival rate for wild tigers is very low. In fact, only one out of every two tigers typically survives to become an adult. There are many reasons for this. The biggest reason is simply that when they are young, tigers are practically helpless. They depend completely on their mothers for survival. While she is out hunting for food, if any other predator comes across them, they may be killed. The same wild dogs that, on rare occasions, will gang up on adult tigers, can easily kill a baby tiger.

A tiger cub plays with a twig. At this age and size, cubs are vulnerable to other predators.

Very often it is other adult tigers that kill the young. If a male wanders by a hidden den of tiger cubs, he will often kill them simply because he knows they may grow up to be rivals for his territory in the future. Also, the adult male tiger knows that the female will not breed with him until she is done raising these cubs. So if he is interested in **breeding** with her, killing the young improves his chances.

The mother tiger is well aware of these dangers to her cubs. She tries not to leave them alone for very long when they are young. She will also fiercely defend the cubs. Most animals that might enjoy snacking on a young tiger cub will do so only when they know the mother tiger is nowhere around. If a lone predator is caught harassing the cubs, it will be chased off or killed by the mother tiger. Even humans have been killed by a female tiger for simply walking, unaware, near a den of cubs. Of course, not all humans chased off by mother tigers are there for completely innocent reasons. In fact, humans are today the single biggest predator of tigers in the world.

A Kink in the Circle

While the tiger may exist at the top of the food chain, one creature basically lives outside the food chain: humans. Humans have invented ways of keeping themselves on top. Unfortunately, this often means stepping on those below them. Humans and tigers have had a long history together. Tigers have been hunted for sport for more than three thousand years, as far back as the time of the ancient Egyptians. Some cultures kept lions and tigers in private collections and hunted them for sport with bows and arrows. Romans put them in arenas to battle gladiators. Some Asian courts used them to execute people.

Although some cultures actually have great respect for the tiger, even placing it among their gods, most ancient cultures see it as a dangerous and, in some circumstances, evil creature. Most ancient texts that compared lions and tigers viewed lions as admirable and majestic, whereas tigers were often described as sneaky, cold-blooded

Historically, the Romans used tigers to battle gladiators (top). Tiger hunts continue to this day despite efforts to stop the practice.

killers. Some ancient people went so far as to bait and torture tigers until eventually a trained group of wild dogs would be released to kill them.

Why Were They Hated?

There are a number of reasons why people would hunt tigers, both in the past and today. Sometimes tigers will hunt cows and other farm animals. Because many people in the area where tigers live exist on the money from their farms, they become quite angry when a tiger does this.

In addition, although most tigers do not prey on humans, some do. Most tigers have an innate fear of humans but on occasion, if the tiger is too old or weak to catch its usual prey, it will go after a person. In reality, humans are much easier targets than deer. Researchers have shown that once a tiger has killed a person, it is more likely to try it again. For this reason, many people live in fear of tigers and believe that they must kill them when they see one near their home.

The Human Predator

A far greater reason that humans hunt tigers is for sport and trade in illegal tiger parts. Around the turn of the last century, it was a very popular sport to travel to India and hunt tigers. Wealthy European nobles would stay with Indian **maharajahs**, or kings, who would gladly take them hunting. The maharajah of Suguja reportedly killed 1,150 tigers during his life.

In addition, many Asian cultures still believe that the body parts of a tiger contain mysterious healing properties. For example, in China people make a tea from the powder of crushed tiger bones, believing it gives people strength. The **pelts**, or fur coats, of the tiger are also in demand. Money is very scarce in the part of the world where tigers live. A local **poacher**, or illegal hunter, can make an entire year's salary by killing and selling one tiger. For this reason, people will risk prison and their lives to kill a tiger and sell it to the market.

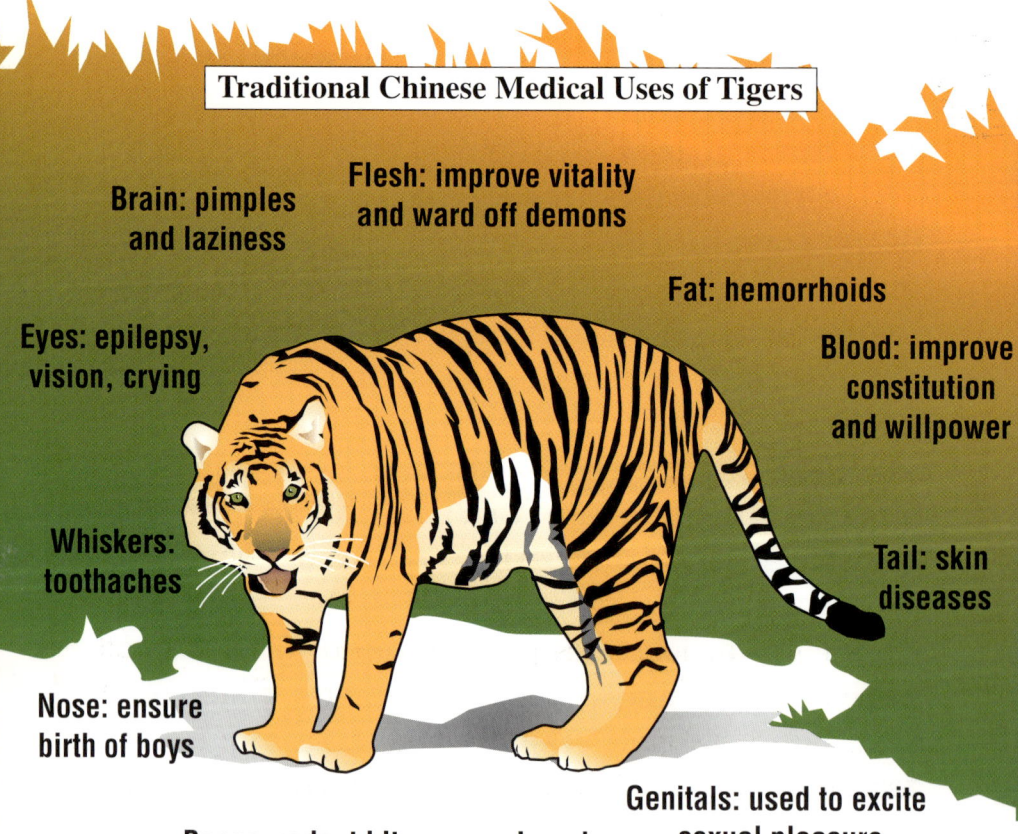

Traditional Chinese Medical Uses of Tigers

Brain: pimples and laziness

Flesh: improve vitality and ward off demons

Fat: hemorrhoids

Eyes: epilepsy, vision, crying

Blood: improve constitution and willpower

Whiskers: toothaches

Tail: skin diseases

Nose: ensure birth of boys

Genitals: used to excite sexual pleasure

Bones: rodent bites, muscle pain, weakness; promote strong bones and teeth

A poacher sells the claws and bones of a tiger in a Chinese marketplace.

Habitat Loss

Perhaps the largest problem for the tiger's survival today is the loss of **habitat**. A habitat is the place where the tiger lives, such as the forests of India, for example. As the number of humans continues to grow, they need to tear down wild places to make room for houses, roads, and even farms to feed themselves. Every time a wild habitat is destroyed, all the animals that live there either die or are forced to move on to a new home. Often they are not able to survive in these new homes and they die a short time later.

In India, for example, the land has changed dramatically. During the 1950s, about 75 percent of the country was covered by forest. Today, these forests make up only 20 percent of the land. This

Indian construction workers use an elephant to help clear a forest area.

adds up to a lot of area lost to tigers and other animals.

Where Does the Tiger Stand Now?

During the beginning of the twentieth century, just over a hundred years ago, there were more than one hundred thousand tigers. Today, there are between five thousand and eight thousand left. Most of these are Bengal tigers. Some of the other types of tigers, such as the Sumatran and Siberian, are extremely **endangered** species, which means that so few are left that no one is sure whether or not they will disappear permanently. In fact, three of the world's eight types of tigers have already become **extinct**. They have completely died off because of hunting and habitat destruction. Once a type of animal disappears from the earth, it is gone forever.

Help Is on the Way

Fortunately, people are starting to notice that tigers are disappearing from the world and are taking steps to prevent it. There is an international list of endangered animals; most countries of the world have agreed not to hunt animals on this list or trade in products made from them.

India became so concerned with the loss of tigers that in 1972, it declared the tiger the national symbol and began a program called Project Tiger. This program had two goals. One goal was to create laws to make sure no one would hunt tigers. The other goal was to protect the tiger's habitat for all time. It accomplished the second goal by choosing nine large forested areas and declaring them as protected national parks. No one is given permission by the government to cut these areas down, so all the tigers that live there are relatively safe.

The Future

Today, people have a lot more respect for the world's largest cat. Efforts such as Project Tiger are being created all over the world to help reverse some of the damage humans have caused. Researchers use

Project Tiger volunteers enter a bungalow that will serve as a base for catching poachers.

many of the same methods that hunters used to track the tigers. However, instead of killing tigers, they study them. By learning about tigers, researchers help the governments and environmental groups of the world figure out better ways to protect them.

In India the number of tigers has increased significantly in the last few decades. The Siberian tiger has also made a big comeback. In the 1930s, as few as thirty individual Siberian tigers were left in the world. Today that number has climbed back up to nearly four hundred. Although these successes are encouraging, there is still much work to be done. The actions of children and adults over the next few decades may forever determine the fate of the tiger.

Glossary

adaptations: Behaviors or parts of an animal's body that help it survive.

breeding: The act of creating young.

carcass: The remains of a dead animal.

crepuscular: Description of an animal that is most active at dawn and dusk.

endangered: When a type of animal's or plant's numbers are so low that they are in danger of disappearing from the world forever.

extinct: When a type of animal or plant has disappeared from the world forever.

food chain: The order of who eats what in the wild.

habitat: The type of wild area that an animal lives in.

maharajahs: Indian kings.

pelts: The skins of a dead animal.

poacher: A person who hunts wild animals illegally.

prey: The animal that a predator will chase and eat for a meal.

semiaquatic: An animal that spends a large part of its life in water.

tapetum: The reflective lining on the back of a tiger's eye that allows it to see at night.

trachea: An animal's windpipe, located in its throat.

For Further Exploration

Fateh Singh Rathore and Valmik Thapar, *Wild Tigers of the Ranthambhore*. New Delhi, India: Oxford University Press, 2000. This book focuses on the lifelong studies of a pair of well-known researchers who have cataloged the lives of a group of Bengal tigers.

John Seidensticker and Susan Lumpkin, *Great Cats*. San Francisco: Fog City Press, 1991. A large coffee table book that provides a light look at the large cats of the world.

Lee Server, *Tigers: Portrait of the Animal World*. New York: Todtri Productions, 1998. This is a comprehensive yet easy-to-read look at the world of the tiger.

Geoffrey C. Ward, "Tigers in Trouble," *National Geographic,* December 1997. A great article explaining some of the current issues facing tiger conservation in the world today.

Art Wolfe and Barbara Sleeper, *Wild Cats of the World*. New York: Crown Publishers, 1995. This beautiful book is a broad overview of most of the world's feline species. It looks at their biology, behavior, and conservation status.

Index